5
SIMPLE
Steps
To A
Debt Free
Life

Jennifer S. Matthews

5 SIMPLE Steps to a Debt Free Life

Copyright © 2017 by Jennifer S. Matthews

Printed in the United States of America

978-0-9986428-0-2

This book is available at quantity discounts for bulk purchases. For information, please direct your inquiries to www.JenniferSMatthews.com

DEDICATION

This book is dedicated to mom and dad for your unconditional love and support, especially during this faith walk as I do my best to humbly answer God's calling.

This book is also dedicated to everyone who reads it. My prayer is that you use the information in this book to 1) reduce any stress your debt may be causing you, and 2) that you get out of debt, stay out of debt, and enjoy living a debt free lifestyle!

To my friends, supporters, and prayer warriors – thank you each so very much!

Table of Contents

FOREWORD

Thank you for picking up my book! I have been helping people stop living paycheck to paycheck for more than ten (10) years. In addition to no longer living paycheck to paycheck, people who work with me increase their savings, get out of debt, raise their credit scores, and position themselves to start living the life of their dreams! I have also incorporated my love of personal development into my work, and that extra benefit has really helped my clients achieve their dreams faster.

I have been successfully teaching people a simple way to get out of debt for many years. I decided to adapt my training into this book so that I could be a resource to more people. Getting out of debt is not complicated, which is why the book is not thick or overwhelming. It takes time, but the steps are very simple. This is a workbook, and *if you do the work you will get the win!* What is the win? Watching your debt decrease until it disappears! No one can do the work for you. This is something you have to commit to doing yourself.

Lowering your debt often lowers your stress. However, one of the greatest benefits of getting out of debt is that your savings increases and you have access to more cash, which means that you have options! Having options is being able to pick and choose what you want to do without financial stress or strain, and that is an awesome position to be in!

Let me say that most people, including me, have had some type of financial issue and/or challenge in their lifetime. The purpose of both of my books is to get you to the point that any debt related stress you have is significantly reduced as your debt is reduced; that you increase your savings; and that you will position yourself to enjoy the numerous options available to each of us during our lives!

In this book, I will show you a simple plan for eliminating all of your debt, including your mortgage. The plan really is simple. However, simple and easy are not synonyms and they definitely are not the same. If most things in life were easy, everyone would have nearly everything they wanted. However, once your commitment to getting out of debt converts to a fire in your belly, the process will become much easier and much faster!

One really cool thing about the fire in your belly is that when life throws you a financial curve (i.e. needing brakes on your car or some other unexpected bill), you will know exactly what to do to overcome come it without derailing your commitment and plan to get out of debt! You will jump over obstacles like an Olympic hurdler! You will blow through stumbling blocks like a professional football player!

This book is short and to the point like my first book, *12 Ways to Put Money in Your Pocket Every Month Without A Part-Time Job*. I worked hard to make it just as powerful and impactful on the life of you, the reader. When you have finished reading and working through this book, you will have a simple written plan to systematically pay off all of your debt. However, it is totally up to you to stick with the plan you create by using the resources you are about to learn. It is also totally up to you to not let "life", unexpected bills, or anything else takes your eye off of *your* prize, which is getting out of debt!

Get ready to achieve! Get ready to succeed!

INTRODUCTION

If you have ever attended one of my live seminars, you know that my style is laid back and that I speak from the heart. Why? Even though I may not know you or your situation, I truly care! My work in the area of personal finances is solely dedicated to providing information and resources to help people create options for themselves and their loved ones.

Too many people are so financially stressed and financially strapped, that they do not have options. What do I mean by options? It is the financial freedom to make rational, comfortable choices to do what you want because the money is available in one of your savings accounts (yes, intentionally plural!). Options become available when you are in control of your finances instead of your finances controlling you. Options may include traveling, going back to school, buying a home, hiring a house cleaner, and so much more! The sky is your limit on options when you are not strapped by debt and you have available savings!

Instead, many people feel like they are trapped by either their finances or their financial situations – and maybe they are. Therefore, they stay at jobs they hate, which is usually not physically and/or emotionally healthy. They work more than one job, which decreases family time and the ability for work/life harmony. They neglect their bodies and go to work sick, or do not take off to go to the doctor because they cannot afford to lose a day of pay, or they cannot afford the cost of the doctor's appointment (or medicine). There are many, many more things that people do not do because they feel financially trapped.

On the flip side, you can choose to do the [sometimes hard] work to get your finances in order and give yourself the opportunity to explore and enjoy options. Having options may improve your health and/or your happiness because you are less stressed. Options may also provide you with the time and financial resources to enjoy new things in life, thereby allowing you to experience a new level of happiness that you may not have achieved yet in your life. Having no debt or minimal debt (i.e. a very affordable mortgage); an adequate emergency fund (preferably 12 months of living expenses); multiple accounts for ongoing savings (i.e. vacations, large purchases (i.e. car or house), tuition, etc.); and a separate account that is growing toward ample retirement income are all keys to creating options for both now and later in your life.

Do not let the previous paragraph discourage you because you may be feeling like you are drowning in debt; that you cannot see any possibilities; and/or that your finances are a wreck and may not be anywhere near anyone of those things, let alone all of them. That's fine! That is why you have this book in your hands! Rome was not built in a day, and each of us rolled over, crawled, and then walked long before we ever ran.

Getting your finances into a position to allow you to take advantage of options in your life may feel like a marathon. Actually, getting out of debt is a marathon and not a sprint! It takes a lot of time, a lot of energy, and a lot of effort. *However*, the victory and the rewards that come with getting out of debt are well worth your investments of time, energy, and effort!

Furthermore, you have this skinny book that walks you through 5 simple steps you can follow to become debt free, increase your savings, and then create cash to use to enjoy your options. Wherever you are on the financial road, the only important thing is that you get started, and then stick with, the plan you create until you start seeing more and more options becoming available in your life!

This book provides you with information and resources for your journey (marathon) to crossing your finish line and being in a strong financial position to take advantage of options. I will also point you to related resources you can explore for additional support and assistance along the way. The one important thing to know is that neither I nor this book can actually do the work needed to change your finances. *You are the only one who can do your work* – even if you are married or in a committed relationship. Your mate cannot do your work for you. No one else can! You have to make the mental commitment and dig deep inside of yourself for the determination to start and then stick with the process. I understand that you may be married and/or have family or other commitments that impact your finances. That's fine. Even if your family members are not supportive, you have to decide that you are doing this for you and for your future.

To help you do the work you need to get out of debt, many chapters end with **A.S.A.P. – A**ction **S**teps toward your **A**ction **P**lan. It is important that you complete each A.S.A.P., and then follow up and follow through on the action.

Here's to your success!

13

1.

DEBT!!! How many of us have it?

DEBT!!! How many of us say we don't want it?
DEBT!!! So what are you going to *do differently this time*?

STACKS OF BILLS!!! DEBT!!! Where the heck did my debt come from? How the heck did I get so much of it? I keep saying I'm going to pay it off, but there's so much of it, and I don't see any progress. Therefore, I don't stick with my thoughts and ideas about paying it off. Sometimes I'm so overwhelmed by my finances, or I feel like I'm in such bad shape, that I decide to ignore it because I just can't see how I can possibly do anything to make it better.

Does any of that sound like you? Am I singing your song? Even worse, in 3 or 4 sentences have I stepped on your toes so much that you want to spend money on a pedicure? The great news is that you are in the right place, at the right time, with the right resource in your hands!

The deep, perplexing question is: are you truly ready to do what it takes for as long as it takes to get out of debt? Understand that if you say yes AND you follow through, you will also lose the stress, anguish, and any other negative emotions that go along with your debt! Now, does that make you feel a whole lot better than the first paragraph of this chapter? If so, keep reading and get ready to work your plan!

As for me, I finally got sick and tired of being sick and tired of my debt. In the midst of it all, I had one bill in particular that raised my blood pressure and stressed me out simply at the sight of the envelope in the mailbox! I knew how high the balance was inside the envelope. I hated it and I hated all the emotions it stirred up each and every month when it came in the mail – just at the sight of the envelope!

One day, I *finally* made a conscious decision to act on that seed of determination that was deep, deep, deep down in the core of my soul. It was time to get out of debt, and do it as fast as I could. My start date was not tied to any tangible date such as a New Year's Resolution, pay increase, etc. My start date was the date I hit my emotional bottom and decided to build my own ladder out of debt – no matter what!

In about three (3) years of focused efforts, my "stress" debt was paid off and my savings had increased for a combined total of more than $50,000...and I did it without being radical. PLUS, the envelope that had been raising my blood pressure every month went to zero! Zilch! Nada! Boy did I celebrate with more than just a happy dance when I made that last payment on that envelope!

Just writing that last sentence made me smile and feel happy all over again! That's where I want you to get to! And, you are welcome to be as radical as you want to be as long as you stay conscientious in your decision making and your actions!

For the purposes of this book, debt and getting out of debt is paying off anything you owe that can be paid to zero and not come back. As an example, utility, phone, and cable bills get paid monthly and come back next month. Recurring bills are expenses, not debt. However, if you are not current on your expenses you can get current by applying the strategies in this book. Another huge benefit of getting out of debt (and current on your expenses) is that your credit scores will go up! That bonus is your "gift" from the financial services industry for you sticking with the steps in this book!

A.S.A.P.

_A_ction _S_teps toward your _A_ction _P_lan

1. Decide if you are truly serious about doing the work needed to get out of debt, _AND_ if you are truly committed to staying debt free

2. Decide how radical you want to be with your debt elimination plan. By radical, I mean how much are you willing to change to get out of debt fast as possible? I was willing to limit social outings that cost money to 2 per month. I still went out, but I found enjoyable things that did not cost money. I also cut back or eliminated a few other things that I was spending money on. However, others are willing to live the complete pauper lifestyle for 12-18 months and smash their debt to zero. You have to decide how fast you want to get out of debt and how radical you are willing to be with your spending so that you can reach your goal!

2.

In the Beginning, There Was No Debt

I believe we need to know where we came from so we can know where we are going. Therefore, let's start with a brief look at how quickly Americans got into debt. I hope this background information will motivate you to do what is needed to get out of debt, and then hopefully stay out of debt. Credit as we know it today started evolving in the 1950s. Credit existed before that time, but only started becoming commercially available in the '50s, and then more and more marketed and accessible by the 1970s. As you read this chapter on how old "credit" is, think about how old you are or how old your parents are.

Prior to the creation of credit cards, loans, and other (now) common and widely available forms of debt, when people could not pay for something at a store they ran a tab or an account with the store owner. This was mainly prior to the 1970s, before supermarkets, the internet, and big box stores. Back then, many stores were small, neighborhood businesses that were individually owned. The owners knew everyone in the community and would keep track of what each person owed for items they needed, but did not have the money to purchase. Typically, when payday came, the customer would pay back what they owed to the store owner. That type of credit was based upon a handwritten record of what was owed and the honesty of a customer's verbal promise to repay.

The emergence and growth of the credit industry were led by the growing desire to purchase cars and homes by more and more people. In the 1950s, cars were still a luxury item but the prices were dropping. However, even though the prices were lower, the price was still too high for most people to purchase a car with cash. Therefore, a credit system was needed to manage the purchases and payments. A credit system was created for people to purchase cars, and that system was soon replicated to allow people to purchase homes.

Diners Club started as a cardboard credit card that was first issued in 1950 with 20,000 members for the sole purpose of dining and entertaining. In 1958, American Express introduced a competing card that was also just for dining and entertainment. The first credit card, named BankAmericard, was also first issued in 1958, but it was only available for local use in California because there were no national banks. At that time, all banks were local or statewide only. Agreements emerged between banks on how multiple banks could use and profit from the BankAmericard, and then BankAmericard became Visa in 1976. Master Charge was introduced in 1966 and was also called the Interbank Card until 1979 when it became MasterCard.

Credit cards did not start becoming truly profitable to banks until 1983-1990, which was during and immediately after the recession of the early 1980s. Credit card rewards did not exist until 1989. The introduction of rewards and reward points made more people want to use credit cards in the 1990s. It was in the late 1980s and early 1990s that banks realized how much profit they could make by adding fees to credit cards, and they particularly targeted cardholders who carried a balance over on their cards from month to month.

Since credit as we know it is relatively new (existing about 60 years), it should not be a surprise that it led the way for the creation of two of the three primary credit bureaus. Transunion started in 1968 and Experian started in 1980. Equifax actually started in 1899 as the Retail Credit Company. The Retail Credit Company got their start by keeping a list of customers and their creditworthiness for the local Retail Grocer's Association.

As a population, in a few short decades, Americans have evolved from using credit to purchase major items like cars and houses (the 1960s), to using credit for convenience purchases and emotional purchases (the 1990s). There are even people who use their credit cards as "status" symbols. Think about gold, silver, platinum, black, premier, and other cards marketed as being "elite" cards. For example, I just *knew* I was hot stuff when I got my gold credit card! My ego swelled every time I took it out and flashed it in the store! I know someone reading this can relate to that feeling...way back in the 1990s!

It is the use of credit for convenience and to soothe or satisfy our emotions that have gotten and/or kept many of us (myself included!) in debt. Some reading this book may feel that you have "manageable" debt, while other readers are feeling overwhelmed, drowning, and even haunted by their debt. If you follow the information and every action step in this book, you will see your progress and watch your balances go down as you get out of debt!

To help keep your debt down both now and going forward, opt out of credit card offers to limit the temptation that comes your way. Plus, as a side benefit, you will lower the amount of junk mail you get! To opt out of credit card offers for five years, call toll-free 1-888-5-OPT-OUT (1-888-567-8688) or visit www.optoutprescreen.com. The phone number and website are operated by the major consumer reporting companies (credit bureaus).

A.S.A.P.

Action Steps toward your Action Plan

1. Being completely honest with yourself, if you think back over your debt, how often do you think you used credit and/or credit cards for status, for convenience, and/or to soothe or satisfy your emotions? Journal your answers.

2. Next, think about how you will overcome these thoughts, feelings, and/or emotions going forward. Getting out of debt is a process, and part of the process is a lifestyle change. You have committed to doing the work to get out of debt. Therefore, it is important to know up front how you are going to keep yourself from going back into debt to buy things that you truly do not need!

3. Opt out of credit card offers by calling 1-888-5-OPT-OUT (1-888-567-8688) or visiting www.optoutprescreen.com.

3.

Why Bother Getting Out of Debt?

Why should you even bother getting out of debt? Truthfully, I really do not know the answer! The answer to that question is personal to you and you alone. What is *your* reason for wanting to be debt free? Why do you want to take the time and put forth the hard work needed to get out of debt? Is it so that you can...

- Lower your stress level?
- Raise your credit scores?
- Have extra money to travel, save for retirement, etc.?
- Put your children or grandchildren through college without loans?
- Be FREE? What does "free" mean to you?
- ... (you write this sentence)

The reason(s) are personal and specific to everyone reading this book. If you read my first book, you know that I am all about taking action and also believe in doing the work needed to get the job done right! Therefore, it is critically important that you stop right now and write down the answers to these two questions:

1. Why do you want to get out debt? To get to the real root reason, ask yourself "why" to whatever you

first write down, and then write your second answer. Ask yourself "why" to your second and subsequent answers. You may be surprised by the real reason that is hiding deep down inside of you!

2. How will you feel when you pay off your last bill and all of your unwanted debt is gone?

Having the answers to these two questions in writing is critically important. Next, post copies of your answers in multiple visible places such as at home, in your wallet, at work, on the dashboard of your car, etc. Even with the simple plan you are about to create with this book, getting out of debt is not complicated, but it also is not easy. It is not easy because most people do not want to take the time to work through their plan while waiting out the process, even though getting out of debt is a very achievable goal even if you have really high credit card and/or loan balances.

If getting out of debt was easy, the majority of people would not have any debt, especially credit cards and personal loans. When you are in the midst of following your debt elimination plan and you feel like you are not making progress or your favorite store is having the "ultimate" sale, you need to go back and reread the reasons you just wrote for wanting to become debt free. This is why you purposely posted your reasons "why" in visible places as a continuous reminder to yourself of what you are doing and, more importantly, why you are doing it. This is one of your motivations! Seeing and reading your reason "why" every day, and especially on challenging days, is what will help you: stay on track through the rough times; defy the negative thoughts that creep into your mind; and keep your commitment to yourself to get out of debt when tests, challenges, temptations, and frustrations come your way – because they are on their way!

From 2010 – 2013, the average household debt decreased which is great – especially if you are one of those households! Depending upon what source you look at, the average household credit card debt varies. A 2014 finance article found that 42.4% of people had credit card debt, and it listed the amounts debt as follows:[1]

- $10,902 to $15,191 average household credit card debt
- $8,864 average credit card balance for millennials
- $12,026 average credit card balance for Generation X

These figures do not include student loan debt or medical bills. These numbers just look at credit cards, which is consumer debt. By consumer debt, I mean the "stuff" people buy. Some stuff you need, and most stuff you probably do not need but you *want* it (if you are completely honest with yourself).

When you buy the stuff you need, such as new brakes or groceries, with a credit card and then do not pay it off at the end of the month, the purchase was probably due to poor planning. Why poor planning when you truly needed brakes for your car? If you own a car, brakes and tires are routine

---

[1] Article: Is Your Credit Card Debt Average? And What is Average? by Michelle Lerner. June 11, 2014.
http://www.dailyfinance.com/2014/06/11/is-your-credit-card-debt-average/

maintenance and should be accounted for in your budget or savings plan. If you live in a cold climate, eventually your winter coat is going to wear out and need replacing. If you own a house, the heat, air conditioner, roof, etc. will need routine maintenance, and eventually replacing.

In the last paragraph, I used the word *budget*, which is the dreaded "B" word for many people. Then, I used the budget in the same sentence as *savings*, and many people think they do not have extra money to put toward savings. If you think that you cannot afford to save, then you need to keep reading! The great news is that the system for getting out of debt explained in this book works on all debt that can be paid to zero and permanently eliminated. Additionally, this book also provides insights and answers to some the concerns and questions you may be having around budgeting and being able to start saving.

A.S.A.P.

Action Steps toward your Action Plan

1. What is your reason for wanting to be debt free? Why do you want to get out debt? To get to the real root reason, ask yourself "why" to whatever you first write down, and then write your second answer. Ask yourself "why" to your second and subsequent answers and you may be surprised by the reason that hiding deep down inside of you!

2. Why do you want to take the time and put forth the hard work needed to get out of debt?

3. How will you feel when you pay off your last bill and all of your unwanted debt is eliminated? This is your goal and your dream! Therefore, one-word answers like awesome, relieved, and happy are not enough!

4.

Rules for Today's Economy

The Critical Importance of Cash (in Your Life and in Your Bank Account)

In our society, many people have replaced using cash with credit cards, loans, and other forms debt. Businesses spend millions of dollars on advertising that convinces us that we have to buy their items. All of the easily available credit makes those purchases possible even when we do not have enough cash for the purchase. Additionally, peer pressure from family, friends, and even society also puts stress on us to buy more "stuff" so that we look or feel like we "fit in". These pressures are also true for our children because we want them to fit in and have the latest and greatest "stuff" even if we, as their parents, cannot afford it.

I believe that cash is king and credit (scores) is queen. Whether you are male or female, you want to be king of your life and accumulate as much cash as possible! When I say this, I do not mean for you to walk around with loads of cash in your purse or pocket. Generally, you should only carry the amount of cash that you are comfortable with, and use debit cards instead of credit cards. You also want to accumulate as much cash savings as possible and work with a licensed financial professional for guidance on investing it based upon your needs, goals, and your risk tolerance.

Cash is king means that it is important for everyone to accumulate cash. By accumulating cash, I am not suggesting that you are or have to become greedy. It is a fact that people are living longer, and far too many seniors do not have enough savings available. Some seniors struggle to make ends meet. Some live in substandard housing and have to choose between buying medicine and buying food. Assistance programs are not available to all seniors, and are often not enough to bridge the financial gap every month. Since none of us can predict our future or our future needs, it is important that we save as much as we can toward that unknown.

Everyone should have two types of savings accounts, short-term and long-term. Throughout this book, you will be encouraged to put some money into short-term savings accounts. It is also very important that as you get out of debt and start to free up larger amounts of cash, that you start building your long-term savings accounts. I do not provide financial or investment advice. Therefore, I strongly encourage you to seek the guidance of a licensed financial professional for assistance with developing a financial plan that meets your current and projected needs.

Having no debt, while building your robust long-term savings plan, does not mean you will be broke with no money available to enjoy actively living your current life. Actually, you will probably have more enjoyment in your life because you should have much less financial stress related to your future, and you will have cash in short-term savings for vacations and "stuff" you want, *and* you will be able to pay cash for it! Therefore, remember that cash is king and you want to be among the people with enough cash for all of your long-term future needs!

The second half of the fabulous financial duo is: credit scores are queen. Your credit scores are vitally important numbers in your daily life. Your credit scores determine how much your debt (i.e. credit and loans) will cost you. FICO® is the most common credit score, and the scores range from 300 – 850. I suggest setting a goal of getting your credit scores over 700, preferably over 740. Know that over time you can achieve this goal regardless of what your credit scores are now. As an awesome bonus, as you are getting out of debt your credit scores should increase!

There are three (3) primary credit bureaus that report credit scores: Equifax, Experian, and Transunion. The higher your credit score, the lower your interest rates will be when you borrow money (mortgage, car loan, credit cards, etc.). When your interest rate is lower, you pay less interest over the life of the debt and that saves you money!

On the flip side, the lower your credit score, the higher your interest rate. When your interest rate is higher, your payments are higher and you pay more money over the life of your debt than someone who has higher credit scores. Additionally, when you are required to make higher payments on one or more of your debts because of low credit scores, you have less cash available every month for you and your family.

	Credit Card Balance	Interest Rate	Minimum Payment
High Credit Scores	$5,000	10%	$ 91.67
Low Credit Scores	$5,000	29%	$170.83
	Difference		**$ 79.16**

(x12 months = $949.92 per year)

	Mortgage Amount	Interest Rate	Minimum Payment
High Credit Scores	$200,000	4%	$ 954.83
Low Credit Scores	$200,000	6.5%	$1,264.14
	Difference		**$ 309.31**

(x12 months = $3,711.72 per year)

(Note: These are examples for illustration purposes only. People with high credit scores can have high-interest rates, especially on credit cards if they missed payments or their balance went over their limit)

In this example, the person with high credit scores has an extra $388.47 ($79.16 + $309.31) every month, which is $4,661.64 per year, after paying the same two bills as the person with low credit scores! What could you do with an extra $390 every month or $4,600 per year? Would that help you get out of debt faster? Would that increase your savings?

Could you do something you have always wanted to do, like take your dream vacation?

Additionally, low credit scores often determine where you can live. A credit report is part of both the rental and mortgage application processes. If your credit scores are too low, then your rental application to live where you want to live may be declined. Likewise, your mortgage application may be denied for the house you fell in love with in the perfect neighborhood with the great schools.

So what can you do to raise your credit scores? Plenty! Most people do not realize that 65% of our credit scores are totally within our control! Your credit scores will probably increase just by consistently doing all of the action steps in this book to lower your debt. Here are the five components of a credit score:

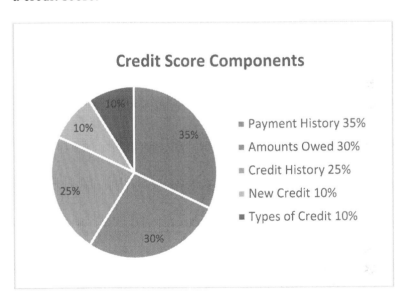

Credit Score Components

- Payment History 35%
- Amounts Owed 30%
- Credit History 25%
- New Credit 10%
- Types of Credit 10%

If you add the two largest credit score components together, Payment History and Amounts Owed, the total is 65%. Payment History is 35% of your credit score. Payment History accounts for whether or not you pay your bills on time. On time means your total payment of the minimum amount due or more is posted to your account on or before the payment due date. One of the best ways to increase your credit scores is to consistently make on-time payments on all of your bills each and every month.

If money is really tight and right now you truly cannot pay all of your bills on time, do not be discouraged! Pick one bill and consistently pay it on time every month. As you work through this book and start creating more cash from within your current income, start paying a second bill on time along with the first bill. Keep adding on-time bill payments until you are paying all of your bills on time every month. You will get there!

The Amounts Owed is 30% of your credit score. There are several debt ratios and each has a slightly different definition and different use. For the purposes of this book, the debt ratio is the Amount Owed on your credit cards compared to your credit limit. Basically, it is the percent of your outstanding balance and your available credit limit. Therefore, if your credit cards are maxed out, or you keep a high balance that is near your credit limit, you are lowering your credit score (see example below).

$6,000 Credit Card Limit		
Outstanding Balance	**Debt Ratio**	**Impact on Credit Score**
$3,500 and up	more than 50%	Bad
$3,000	= 50%	Fair
$2,000 and less	less than 33% (1/3)	*Good*
~ zero ~		*~ Best ~*

As a target, the difference between the amount owed that you do not pay off on a credit card and your credit limit should be 33% (1/3) or less so that you do not lower your credit scores. In the example above, 1/3 of a $6,000 credit limit is $2,000. Therefore, keeping any unpaid monthly balance under $2,000 will help your credit scores. This is where doing the work to get out debt will really benefit you! When you make on-time payments while you are working to get out of debt, the 65% of your credit score that is in your control is a slam dunk and you will win with increased credit scores! Keep reading this book and working on your debt elimination plan so that your efforts can maximize the positive impact on your credit scores!

If you want or need more information on understanding and increasing your credit scores, or more information on the five credit score components, there is an abundance of information available online. Government backed websites include the Federal Trade Commission, AnnualCreditReport.com, and the Consumer Financial Protection Bureau. Also, visit your local library for books. I never suggest or recommend paying for credit repair services. Improving credit scores is a lifestyle change that consists of *always* making on time payments, and having either low or zero credit card and loan balances.

Correcting any errors on your credit reports is something you can do yourself. The Federal Trade Commission (FTC) published a free booklet to help consumers understand and increase their credit scores. You can download the FTC's free booklet from my website, www.PositiveFinancialImpactNOW.com. By making a commitment to consistently use each of the principles in this book, you are committing to a major component of the lifestyle change necessary to increase your credit scores.

If you choose to use a credit repair company (non-profit or for profit) instead of doing the work to repair your credit yourself, do your research first because there are probably as many scammers out there as there are legitimate businesses. However, if you are not fully committed to paying your bills on time and keeping your credit card balances low, then you are simply wasting your money because those two actions are still 65% of your credit score!

A.S.A.P.

Action Steps toward your Action Plan

1. Get at least one copy of your credit report from www.AnnualCreditReport.com. You can get one free copy of each of your credit reports every 12 months. The report is free, and it cost less than $10 to get your credit score. If you have not seen your credit score in the past 12 months, get at least one credit score. **NOTE**: Only access websites like AnnualCreditReport.com and other sites that need your personal information using a private, secure internet connection. I do not recommend using public internet connections such as libraries, cafes, restaurants, or hotels to access your credit reports or any websites that contain your secure/sensitive information.

2. Review your credit reports for errors. If your credit report has debts listed that are not yours or has entries that are incorrect, download the Federal Trade Commission's free booklet on understanding credit because it contains a section on how to dispute errors on credit reports. The booklet is available at www.FTC.gov and on my website www.PositiveFinancialImpactNOW.com. You can also find information on how to dispute errors on each of the credit bureau websites (Equifax, Experian, and the TransUnion).

3. Hold on to your credit report(s). Your credit report is a critical step in your upcoming debt elimination plan!

5.

What Does Your Family Have to Do With This?

Is Your Past Part of Your Present?

Many people try to put their past behind them. However, when it comes to managing your money and getting out of debt, knowing and understanding your past will help you with your present goal of getting out of debt.

If you are beating yourself up because of your past decision making and/or events that contributed to your current financial/debt situation, please stop! Instead, you should be congratulating yourself for your determination to change your situation and get out of debt. If you are like most people, managing money was not openly discussed when you were growing up. Therefore, you were probably not taught the importance of saving; how to budget; how to balance your checkbook; or other important financial keys for everyday living. However, depending on how you were raised, your childhood could have left you with more than just not learning basic keys to having a good financial foundation.

For some people, as a child money was a very negative subject in their home. Perhaps you remember lots of arguments about money. Perhaps you remember being denied things you wanted or needed because there was not enough money. Perhaps you remember being told that money does not grow on trees. Perhaps you were punished for something related to money. Perhaps you were teased because you were not able to wear the latest styles and trends. Perhaps all of your friends were going to do something and your family did not have the money for you to participate so you were left out.

How has this impacted your view of money in adulthood? How has your past contributed to the way you handle money today? Do you hoard money so you will never be without it again? Do you spend lavishly to make up for the things you were denied growing up? Do you ignore money/money management because of something in your past?

Perhaps your experience growing up was positive or even extravagant. Perhaps there were no money concerns in your house so you never thought about it because whatever you needed or wanted always appeared. Perhaps you got almost everything you asked for because money was not an issue in your home. How has this impacted your view of money? How has your past contributed to the way you handle money today? Is part of your debt from trying to maintain a past image or lifestyle that your current income cannot sustain?

Based upon your past experiences with money, whether positive or negative, has it impacted how you interact with your spouse, children, and even your friends? Do you and your spouse openly talk (not argue) about money and work together toward clearly defined, mutually agreed upon financial goals? Do you teach your children how to understand money and to be responsible with it?

Understanding the impact of your past on your present financial situation is critically important work that goes beyond the pages of this book. My goal in these last few paragraphs is to create awareness that there may be some hidden contributors to your debt and your mindset about money that you may not be aware of. Knowledge is power. As you gain knowledge and insight into the impact of your past (financial upbringing) on your present (current financial situation), you can work to change your mindset, behaviors, perceptions, and actions around money. For additional information and resources to assist you, sign up for my mailing list at www.PositiveFinancialImpactNOW.com. You can also search the internet for articles and books on money mindset.

6.

The Balancing Act!

So many people tell me that math is hard or that they hate math! After you get out of debt, you are going to have a good amount of cash that you will want (and need) to count and watch multiply, which is where the fun comes in. With that said, I suggest you start practicing your "money accumulation math" now so that you are an expert at it when you start having extra cash to count!

If you are still having anguish at the thought of math, think about it this way... When you walk into your favorite store and they are having a sale, do you head to the 10% off rack or do you make a beeline for the 33%, 50%, or 75% off racks? I like to think of math as a scale. When the scale tip in my favor, such as a great sale or money growing my bank account, then math is easy and counting is fun! However, if you're talking about taxes or complex formulas and algorithms, then I will leave that kind of math to those who enjoy it.

You can do *some* (a little!) shopping with the debt elimination plan you will create with this book (some debt books barely let you breathe and you definitely cannot spend money!), and your savings will be growing as you are getting out of debt. Therefore, it is best to get started with the necessary math now instead of waiting. Plus, as you get out of debt, the money you have will start to multiply and grow in your savings accounts. That is the fun, money accumulation math that you will look forward to calculating! Don't worry! The math needed to get out of debt is much, much easier than calculating the additional 60% off the shirt you want that is on sale now for $23.50.

One of the most important steps in getting out of debt is knowing how much money you have available to work with. Millions of people do not balance their checkbook, and therefore do not know how much money they have. Additionally, these people are at an increased risk of overdraft fees. Overdraft fees are a completely preventable waste of your hard earned cash! If you bounce an average of five checks a year with an overdraft fee of $35, you waste $175 every year. However, there are people who bounce 4 or 5 checks *every month*!

As part of your work to get out of debt, *you have to start balancing your checkbook immediately!* It is critical that you know how much money you have every pay period or every month to pay your current bills and expenses, and to use to get out of debt. Balancing your checkbook will also allow you to track the additional money you will create using the information in this book. It is very important that you track all of your money because, if you do, you will get out of debt faster.

If you are already faithfully balancing your checkbook – congrats to you and keep it up! For everyone else, balancing your checkbook is simple addition and subtraction. You can do the math in your head, with a calculator, on your phone, tablet, or use whatever device you choose as long as you do it.

I have purposely not mentioned apps and websites that help balance checkbooks, keep track of bills, and provide other support. There are more apps and websites out there than I could possibly review or keep up with. If you think apps will be of value to you, do your research to make sure that whatever you choose is both credible and has the protections in place to keep your information and data secure.

However, as someone just getting started on the journey to becoming debt free, I suggest you do the math and track your money yourself (without apps or tracking websites) for at least the first 6 – 8 months of your commitment to becoming debt free.

A.S.A.P.

Action Steps toward your Action Plan

1. You guessed it! If you do not balance your checkbook, that is your immediate action step! Knowing how much money you have at all times will help you get out of debt faster. Balancing your checkbook is simple addition and subtraction that is critical for your success!

2. Review your bank statements for the last 12 months and add up any overdraft fees. Make a commitment to yourself to keep your checkbook balanced and avoid wasting money on overdraft fees! If you have been charged other banking fees, identify why and then work toward eliminating those fees going forward.

7.

Who and How Much Do You Owe?

Starting Your Debt Elimination Plan

One of the most important things you need to know to get out of debt is the total amount of debt you have, and who your creditors are. It sounds simple, and maybe even sounds like common sense but many people *think* they know how much debt they actually have but they are wrong! Whether you are sure about your total debt amount, think you know your amount, or have no clue about how much debt you have – you need to follow these steps!

To be most effective at getting out of debt and to avoid future surprises, you need to know who you owe and how much you owe to each creditor (the institution or person you borrowed money from). You will not be able to design an accurate debt elimination plan without this exact information. There are two primary resources to help you with this.

First, review the last six months entries in your checkbook register. If you pay your bills online, download your records for your last six months of bill payments. From these resources, write down the name of each creditor with an outstanding balance that can be permanently eliminated. For example, your rent, utility bills, and phone bills get paid each month and are recurring every month so they cannot be eliminated. However, credit cards, medical bills, and loans (including your mortgage) can be paid off and permanently eliminated, which is your goal.

Next, if you do not have a recent bill with the total outstanding balance, call each creditor or log into each account and write down the total outstanding balance for each debt that can be eliminated. Writing down each outstanding balance is critical for the debt elimination plan you will be creating shortly.

The second resource for identifying your debt are your credit reports. There may be debts on your credit reports that you are not aware of, or that are on your reports in error. Start by getting a copy of at least one of your credit reports for free at www.AnnualCreditReport.com. This is the official government backed website for consumers to get a free copy of their credit reports once every 12 months. The credit report is free, but there is a small fee if you want your credit score.

You have three credit reports and each one, including each credit score, is probably different. The reports are different because not all creditors report your information to all three credit bureaus. It is not uncommon for the range of a person's three credit scores to differ by 50 or even 100 points. You only need one credit report to create your debt elimination plan. However, if you are truly committed to getting out of debt, I suggest you get all three reports so that you do not miss any debts you may have. If you already have one or more of your credit reports, and they are not more than about 12 months old, you can use them and do not need to get a newer copy.

In chapter 4, I provided a brief overview on credit (Credit is Queen). You do not need your credit score(s) to create your debt elimination plan. However, your credit scores will probably go up as your debt goes down. Having at least one credit score before you start eliminating your debts will allow you to see your scores increase. There are numerous websites and resources that offer free credit reports. Know that for many of these offerings there may be strings attached or something buried in the fine print that could cost you in the long run, so beware! For those reasons, I suggest you only use www.AnnualCreditReport.com to get free copies of your credit reports.

Once you have your credit report, read it carefully and mark each account that is currently open and has a balance. If the account is current or is less than three (3) years past due, write down the name of the creditor and the total outstanding balance. For accounts that are more than three (3) years past due and/or are charged off, do some research online with reputable resources and also read books from your local library to determine the best course of action *for you* for these older debts.

There are many fraudulent credit repair offers on the market. To protect yourself, I suggest only using government resources such as the FTC or government-sanctioned organizations such as the housing counseling agencies listed on HUD.gov. Many HUD-approved housing counseling agencies offer legitimate free or low-cost credit repair services, and also provide financial counseling to help you sustain the outcome of the services they provided to you.

Let's get back to the list of debts you made from your records of bills you paid and your credit reports. This list is what you will use to create your debt elimination plan. Add to your list any money that you borrowed from anyone and have not yet paid back. Also, list any other money you owe that may not be listed in your checkbook register or on your credit report.

Look at your list and add up your total. Is your total debt about what you thought it was? Or, is it higher? Is it lower? Take a moment to think about how you will feel when half of these debts have been totally eliminated and you are working on the few that remain!! I am being serious! Stop, close your eyes, and picture how you will feel! Write your feelings down with today's date at the top of the page.

Every day you should already be reading the reason you wrote down for WHY you are committed to getting out of debt. Then, every 2 – 3 months, you are going to refer back to the paper that reveals how you will feel when your total debt balance is half of what it is today. This will be yet another motivational tool to help keep you focused on your goal, and to keep you encouraged as you are getting closer to being totally debt free!

You should also refer back to both of these pages on the days when you are struggling and want to quit your debt elimination plan or go off track by making a big, unnecessary purchase. Know that setbacks, stress, and frustrations will occur during the time it takes to get out of debt. You will definitely overcome them; however, the goal is to overcome them without adding to your debt and with minimal stress.

A.S.A.P.

Action Steps toward your Action Plan

1. If you have not already downloaded your credit report, do that now at AnnualCreditReport.com. Also, review your report(s) and dispute any errors you find.

2. Review the last six (6) months of bills paid using your *(balanced!)* checkbook register, online bill payment records, and your credit report(s).

3. Write a list of your debts (who you owe) from your records of bills you paid and your credit reports. Add to your list any money that you borrowed from anyone and have not yet paid back. Also, list any other money you owe that may not be listed in your checkbook register or on your credit report.

8.

Creating Your Spending Plan

To get out of debt, you have to create a plan for how you will spend your money from this day forward. While you are working to get out of debt, how you spend every dollar that comes into your possession is critically important. You have to plan what you spend your money on so that you will know if you have extra money to apply to your debt elimination plan and to add to your short-term savings account. Any extra money applied to your debt elimination plan will get you out of debt faster! Do not worry because *even with a spending plan you will still be able to enjoy* an occasional super latte special, go to the movies, and do other things you enjoy. However, you will simply take a little time in advance to plan the money you spend on purchases and outings.

Think about how many things you have planned in your life. I have planned vacations, parties, events, and more. We plan weddings, changing jobs, how we will get from point A to point B, dinner with that special someone, and so many other events, occasions, and activities.

However, when it comes to our money, most of us spend little or no time planning how we will spend our life-sustaining, life-enjoying income. It is the income we earn from working, and that we get from other sources, that funds everything we do – from the roof over our heads and necessities, to buying a latte, to going on vacation, and more. It is important to know and understand that the more we plan how we spend our income, the farther the income we have will go! You will be shocked and amazed at how much *more* you will be able to do with the same amount of income just because you took a little time up front to plan your spending!

Get started by going online and downloading a spending plan template. I purposely wrote a few paragraphs in this chapter before I used the word "budget". A spending plan and a budget are the same except that "spending plan" is a more accurate description of what you are really doing when you write out how you will spend your money. Plus, you are already used to planning things in your life. Now you are just planning one more thing – but it is *the* one thing that will truly change your future for the better!

The spending plan template allows you to list all of your income and expenses, and then total them. There is a free spending plan template on my website, www.PositiveFinancialImpactNOW.com, and there are numerous other template styles readily available in your favorite search engine. The spending plan template on my website is a simple Excel spreadsheet with the formulas already included so that the user does not have to do any math.

It is important that you list all of your income and each of your expenses in the template. If your income is not steady, such as commission sales and self-employment, list your average monthly income. List all of your expenses, not just the debts you will focus on eliminating. Make sure you include expenses that you may not pay every month such as the water and sewer bills and car insurance.

For any occasional expenses you have, list the average amount that you would pay each month if it was a monthly bill. For example, if your water bill is $90 every three months, then that is an average of $30 per month ($90 divided by three months). If your car insurance is $700 every six months, then the average is $116.67 per month ($700 divided by six months).

If you get child support or alimony and it's steady, include it in your spreadsheet unless you are already faithfully putting 100% of it into savings upon receipt. If your child support or alimony is not steady or dependable, do not include it. Make it one of your goals to use the information in this book to create enough extra money from within your existing income to pay all of your bills without the sporadic alimony or child support. That way when you do receive it, you can add all of it to your savings or direct some of it to your debt elimination plan.

If you can use your spending plan to plan your spending in a way that you no longer need the alimony or child support (or any other sporadic income sources) to make ends meet during the month, you will not be financially stressed if you do not receive that income! If you are dependent upon an undependable income source, then I hope that thought put a smile on your face!

Back to your spending plan...When you complete your first one, it is pretty common for the bottom line to be negative, meaning that you have more bills than income each month or each pay period. In my live workshops, I always tell the audience that I am one of the few financial leaders who will tell you that it is actually OK! Yes, it really is OK to have more expenses than income when you *first start* writing out your spending plan.

Writing down your income and expenses is a critically important step in your journey to becoming debt free. Most humans are visual; therefore, we need to "see" so that we can "do" better. Yet, we are also afraid to face the facts because the numbers do not lie. Therefore, for those reasons and a bucket full of other excuses (my favorite: *"I already know I have more bills than money, so I don't need to write it down"*), we avoid writing out our spending plans.

However, it is impossible to fix what you cannot see! How are you going to plan your spending so that you can get out debt if you cannot see what you are currently spending your money on? How are you going to get out of debt if you do not know who you owe or how much you owe? You have to write it down. ***You have to do the work to get your win.***

Having more bills than money when you write down your initial spending plan is OK because your first victory happens when you overcome all of your negative self-talk and write your spending plan down anyway! As you work through the processes in this book, which includes updating your spending plan every month, you will start to see the gap between your income and expenses start to close! Imagine if you set a goal that 12 months from now you will have money left over every month after paying your bills...and you achieve it because you spend the year keeping up with the processes outlined in this book. *It will happen* if you stick with the processes every day, especially on the hard days!

Getting out of debt and changing your financial future is a process that will happen over time when you do the work. If you have taken the time to do everything I have asked of you so far, you need to fold your arms across your chest and squeeze hard to give yourself a BIG hug...because you deserve it! Understand that it took time for your debt and general finances to get to the point that you chose to pick up this book. Likewise, it will take time for you to get your finances to where you want them to be, including becoming debt free. Know that next year is coming and you cannot stop it. The question is: will you be in the same financial situation next year, or will you spend the next 12 months actively working on your commitment to yourself and your family to make sure your financial situation is much better?

It is important that you rewrite your spending plan every month because it should not be the same! The money tracking activity (spending journal) in this book, combined with the excitement you will have as you start watching your debts go down, will help make a difference every month. I expect that you will turn a corner and start getting fired up about paying down your debt! As you keep writing your spending plan every month, the gap between your income and expenses will close, and your debt balances will be going down as well.

Since writing your spending plan every month is critically important, set a reminder on your phone, calendar, computer, or on a system that will notify you. Write your spending plan to correspond with the times of the month you get income. After you write your income and expenses, use a calendar to write the following:

- Mark each payday for the upcoming month
- Write in the due date for each expense and bill paid in that month
- Arrange your bills so that you know which ones will be paid out of each paycheck. Do your best to pay all of your bills on time (increasing credit scores!)
- Set aside a fixed amount of spending money for each period between paychecks.

  o Account for groceries, gas/transportation, childcare, etc.
  o Make sure you include the estimated cost of any special occasions that are scheduled during the pay period (i.e. birthdays, anniversaries, etc.)
  o Plan how you spend your allocated spending money because when it's gone, you do not want to go into savings or use credit to cover you until your next payday. [Note: For some people, it is very effective to withdraw the set amount in cash and put it in an envelope. Once the money is gone, that is it! There are no ATM withdrawals, so it helps them to manage the future envelopes better!]

Total your income, expenses, and spending money for each paycheck. If you are short on cash, look for ways to close the gap so that you do not have to use credit cards, savings, or take on new debt including borrowing money. Refer to the money tracking activity (spending journal) you are about to learn for ways to close the gap between your income and expenses.

A.S.A.P.
Action Steps toward your Action Plan

1. If you are not currently actively using a budget or spending plan, go online and download a spending plan template. There is a free spending plan template on my website, www.PositiveFinancialImpactNOW.com, and there are numerous other styles readily available in your favorite search engine.

2. List all of your income and each of your expenses in the template. If your income is not steady, such as commission sales and self-employment, list your average monthly income. List all of your expenses, not just the debts you will focus on eliminating, and include occasional expenses like car insurance, and water and sewer bills.

3. Update your spending plan every month or every pay day.

9.

Disappearing Acts:

Where Does Your Money Go?

We go to work or have some way of generating income, but for most people, it always seems to disappear faster than we can create it! Since you must have money to pay off your debts, you need to know where your current money is going. Once you know where it is going, you can plug any money leaks you identify. As you plug the money leaks, you can then redirect the money that was leaking out and use it to pay down, and then pay off your debt. And yes, it really is just that simple!

In order to know where your money goes so that you can plug your money leaks, you need to track your daily spending. A spending journal is a key component of your work toward getting out of debt for two important reasons. First, keeping a spending journal allows you to track every penny you spend so that you know exactly where all of your money goes. Second, the entries you record in your spending journal should help you find extra money that you can use in your debt elimination plan.

Keeping a spending journal will show you other areas where you can make spending adjustments to create a few extra dollars that you can put toward your debt elimination system. In your spending journal, record all money that leaves your hands, pocket, bank account, etc. The spending journal will reveal your spending habits and any spending patterns.

Get a small notebook (2x3 is fine) to keep in your pocket or purse. It is important that you write down every penny you spend each and every day in your notebook. Write everything from every purchase – whether it's just a quarter in a gumball machine or your mortgage/rent payment! Include money given to your children, church, bills, etc. Record everything, including non-cash purchases and bills paid online, even if you have receipts or other records of the purchases.

Write in your spending journal daily for at least 60 days, but preferably longer. At the end of every week, review the entries in your notebook and circle the items you can adjust and spend less money on the next time (i.e. eating out, unplanned and impulse purchases, etc.). During the following week, work on adjusting how much you spend on each of your circled items while still recording each of your new purchases. Also pay attention to your spending on recurring purchases such as gas, groceries, parking, etc. When you spend less on a purchase than you did in the past, use the money saved to make an extra payment on the target bill in your debt elimination plan.

Here are examples of spending journal notebook entries:

1/5		1/6	
Bagel	3.22	Cleaners	33.20
Lunch	8.78	Shoes	56.99
Happy Hour	11.56	Groceries	42.21
		Happy Hour	14.70
Total:	$23.56		$147.10

1/7		1/8	
Bagel	3.22	Mortgage	33.20
Lunch	11.20	Electric	56.99
Snack	1.59	Cable	42.21
Dinner	8.69	Phone	14.70
		Credit Card	100.00
Total:	$24.70		$1,337.50

1/9		1/10	
Bagel	3.22	Bagel	33.20
Lunch	7.82	Dinner	56.99
D's gift	41.76		
Happy Hour	11.56		
Total:	$64.36		$61.49

Look at these entries. What spending patterns do you see? What are some money leaks that you see? Where was money spent that could be redirected to getting out of debt? In 6 days, $147.05 was spent eating out, even though groceries were purchased. Even if the dinner was a special occasion that is subtracted out, there is still almost $100 spent in less than one week.

If the eating pattern in this example continues for the 30 days in a month, that is about $500 spent every month eating out, with an additional $200 spent on groceries! What if this person cut their eating out in half and only spent $250 per month? That would create an extra $250 every month to pay down their debts while still having money available to enjoy life! How fast would you get out of debt with an extra $250 every month and a written debt elimination plan?! Here is a chart I created for some of the trainings and workshops I give:

The Work Day: Where Does Your Money Go?				
Purchase	Estimated Cost/ Day	Avg/ Week (x5 days)	Avg/ Month (x4 weeks)	Avg/ Yr (x12 mos)
Coffee	$2.00	$10.00	$40.00	$480.00
Breakfast	$4.00	$20.00	$80.00	$960.00
Lunch	$8.00	$40.00	$160.00	$1,920.00
Snacks	$8.00	$10.00	$40.00	$480.00
Bottled Water	$1.50	$7.50	$30.00	$360.00
Cigarettes (7 days)	$6.00	$42.00	$168.00	$2,016.00
TOTALS:	$23.50	$129.50	$518.00	$6,216.00

Take a good, hard look at this example. This is an example of what the work day may look like for someone – and evening and weekend spending is not included here! Do you see yourself in this example? Imagine if this person made coffee and breakfast at home 3 days a week and only purchased them 2 days each week? What if they brought their lunch from home twice and only ate out 3 days? What if they eliminated buying snacks and water every day, and instead purchased them at the grocery or big box store and stored the items at work?

Do you realize that just making these small changes creates over $50 each week, which is more than $200 every month! How much faster will you get out of debt if you had an extra $200 every month to go toward your debt elimination plan? Did you notice that having a spending plan still allows for the ability to eat out, as seen in this example? The spending plan was used to plan to eat out half as much as before having the spending plan, and then the amount saved would be used to get out of debt faster!

If you smoke, STOP! For health reasons, it is the one area that I am firm about going cold turkey! I would rather you initially use the money you create from not buying cigarettes and tobacco products to pay for a good smoking cessation resource. Talk to your medical provider about smoking cessation resources and options that are right for you. Once you no longer need to pay for the smoking cessation resource, put that money into savings or add it to your debt elimination plan.

Now it's your turn. Grab your spending journal notebook and review your entries. Remember that you are going to write your purchases in your notebook every day for 60 days, and then review them every week. Ask yourself the same three questions you just used to review the entries in the spending example: What spending patterns do you see in your notebook this week? What are some money leaks that you see? Where did you spend money that could be redirected to getting out of debt faster?

What are your answers when you are looking at your own notebook entries? At the end of each week, review every purchase for the week. Circle the purchases that were optional, and circle the purchases that can be adjusted or cut back on in the future. Make a serious commitment to yourself that going forward you will cut back on, or even eliminate, the purchases you circled. This is where you have the flexibility to be radical! You can cut your circled spending by at least 50% (the minimum recommended amount), or 75% (go for it!), or by 100% and be totally radical!

Being focused on getting out of debt does not mean you cannot have fun and/or cannot spend money. It simply means that you get in the habit of calculating your spending in advance. However, to get out of debt as fast as possible you will want to be radical and eliminate 90% or more of the optional and unnecessary spending that you identify in your spending journal. Your spending plan and your spending journal are two key places where you are going to find money every month to pay off your debt faster!

If you have children, did your notebook happen to reveal that you gave them an allowance or spending money, and then spent your money on them instead of having them spend the money that you already gave them? This is often an eye opener for parents...and trust me that your children are well aware that you are giving them money and then spending your money on them!

Two important points. First, let your children spend the money you give them (and not yours!). Teach them how to save some and manage the rest. You would probably rather have your 16-year-old run out of money (and you do not give them more!) and learn money lessons while living at home under your roof, then have your 26 or 36-year-old run out of money and get an eviction or foreclosure notice!

It is important *not* to give your children more money after the money that you gave them for an allotted time (i.e. two weeks) runs out. If you run out of money between paychecks, my guess is that you cannot go to your employer and ask for more. Therefore, why set false expectations for your child and teach them money lessons that do not work in the real world? Let your children be "broke" and learn money management while living at home with all of their essential needs provided for them.

Regardless of your child's age, use the times when they run out of money as teachable moments to help them learn how to manage money. There are numerous age-appropriate financial literacy resources online for your children ages 3-18, including MyMoney.gov and the Consumer Financial Protection Bureau's *Money As You*

Grow. Simply use your preferred search engine to locate this and other great curriculum and resources. By reviewing the lessons you find with your children, you will probably pick up a few tips that will either help your finances now or help you stay out of debt later. Plus, you will be setting your children up to better manage their money starting at an early age.

The second point is that your children will benefit from you becoming debt free. Therefore, I do not suggest delaying your debt free date by giving your children extra cash, especially if they did not manage the money you already gave them. There are numerous simple resources online to teach children of all ages how to manage money. Stay focused on eliminating your debt, and start enjoying more (financially) stress-free family time!

Use your spending journal to track your spending adjustments so that you know how much money you create. Even if you only create a few dollars each week or each month, you are making BIG progress! The goal is to apply the money you create to your debt elimination plan so that you will get out of debt faster. You may be able to group some spending into categories that you can work on adjusting. Once you see how you are spending money, then going forward you can make informed decisions about whether to make an unplanned outing or purchase or apply the cost/purchase price toward your debt elimination plan. Remember, getting out of debt is a marathon and not a sprint!

Keeping a spending journal is often a hard activity for most people. Why? Because it puts their spending in front of them in black and white. Usually, people get upset when they see where and how they are spending money. However, spending journals are a critical requirement for shortening your time to becoming debt free!

A.S.A.P.
_A_ction _S_teps toward your _A_ction _P_lan

1. Get a small notebook that fits in most of your pockets or your purse. Start writing down every purchase you make every day regardless of how large or small the purchase, or how you pay for it. This is your spending journal that you will use to track your purchases and spending for at least 60 days.

2. At the end of each week, review your spending journal entries. Circle spending that you can reduce, and look for patterns of spending that you can adjust. Ask yourself these questions:

    a) What spending patterns do you see in your notebook this week?
    b) What are some money leaks that you see?
    c) Where did you spend money that could be redirected to getting out of debt?

3. Use online resources like the Consumer Financial Protection Bureau and your local library to start teaching your children about money and money management.

10.

But It's *JUST* $10!

Writing your spending plan and keeping a spending journal are key ongoing parts of your debt elimination plan. It is important to understand the impact of each part of the plan. If you are like most people, right now you are unsure of your ability to stick to the plan you are creating. How much debt you have; whether or not you will stick with the plan; and/or the impact of your negative emotions around your debt may also be contributing to your uncertainty about your ability to get out of debt. Therefore, I encourage you to keep working and to have blind faith in this process that has worked for millions of people over the years!

It is important that you understand that every single dollar you find, or that you can make available to add to your debt elimination plan, makes a HUGE difference. Here is something from Bank of America's™ website that shows how big of an impact that just finding just an extra $10 every month will have in your debt!

The payoff from paying an extra $10.

The monthly total minimum credit card payment for a Bank of America credit card is 1% of your current balance plus interest charges and any late fees for the month. Let's look at an example that uses a credit card balance of $1,500 and an APR of 18% to illustrate how *increasing your monthly credit card payment to $10 above the total minimum due could save you time and money.*

Paying just the total minimum due: *With an initial minimum payment of $37 per month, it will take 159 months to pay off that $1,500 debt, with a total interest charge during the payback period of $1,760. The total amount paid back for borrowing $1,500 would be $3,260.*

Paying $10 more than the total minimum due: *With a set monthly payment of $47 (the initial $37 due plus just $10 extra), it will take 44 months to pay off your debt, with a total interest charge of $557.59 during the payback period. The total amount paid back would be $2,057.59.*

The potential savings: By paying $10 over the minimum amount due on your credit card every month, and keeping up that fixed payment amount until the debt is fully repaid, you could save $1,202.41 in interest payments.

Additionally, the debt would be paid off 115 months sooner – that's almost 9 ½ years sooner.[2]

---

[2] https://www.bankofamerica.com/credit-cards/education/paying-more-than-minimum-on-credit-cards.go This example is for illustrative purposes only, based on the assumptions described here: Monthly payment is $10 more than initial $37 total minimum payment due and remains at that fixed payment throughout payback period. No new additional debt is added to the starting balance. Account terms vary and

There are several important things to look at in this example of what *just* an extra $10 per month will do for your debt elimination goal. Making the minimum payment takes 159 months, which is 13 years to pay off $1,500, plus paying more in interest than the initial balance! However, when you look at what happens when you find *just* $10 every month, in this example the total time to pay off the balance drops to 3 ½ years and there's a savings of $1,200 in interest that does not get paid and stays in your pocket instead!

When used consistently and honestly (do not cheat on yourself!), your written spending journal and spending plan will show you how to create far more than *just* $10 every month! The power of applying the extra money you create to your debt elimination plan every month will get you out of debt faster. I hope you see the opportunity and importance of using your spending journal and spending plan to find money, and the importance of creating and then sticking with your debt elimination plan. I have confidence that you can and will use the simplicity of this book to get out of debt and completely change your future!

If you add up all the money your spending journal shows that you either saved or did not spend every week, I am very confident that it will add up to much more than $10 especially by the end of each month! Once you know your total amount of money created for the week, it is important to apply it to your target debt in your debt elimination plan. If you pay your bills online, you can make additional payments each week on your target bill as identified in your debt

---

this example may work differently based on the specific terms of your account.

elimination system. If you pay your bills with a check, move the extra money into a separate savings account until it is time for you to pay your bills. Then, move the money into your checking account and add the amount to your scheduled payment on your target bill.

Before you start making multiple monthly payments on any bill, it is very important that you read the fine print to make sure there are no fees and/or penalties for making multiple payments in the same month. Do not make assumptions. Remember from chapter 2 that creditors are in the business of making money, so there is the possibility of fees being charged for making multiple payments in the same month and/or for paying some loans off early. Make sure you either read the fine print for your account type, or call the creditor, or do both.

The first time I kept a spending journal, was about 25 years ago. I was stunned at how much money I spent every week eating out! Being young and single, sometimes I ate out 7-10 times in one week! If you think of an average of $5 per meal (back then!), that was $35 - $50 in one week. However, there are four weeks in a month so the amount I spent could easily have been $140 - $200 every month, which is far more than *just* $10! If you use your spending plan and your spending journal to create this kind of extra money, how much faster do you think you will reach your goal of getting out of debt? I am truly excited for you!

If you are still having trouble closing the gap between your income and expenses, get a copy of my first book, *12 Ways to Put Money in Your Pocket Every Month Without A*

Part Time Job: The Skinny Book That Makes Your Wallet Fat for more ways to create income from your current income. It is an award-winning, best-selling book. Most readers create $300 - $500 per month from within their current income by following the steps in the book. Get your copy on my website: www.PositiveFinancialImpactNOW.com (these copies are autographed), at online booksellers, and at some retail locations.

A.S.A.P.
*A*ction *S*teps toward your *A*ction *P*lan

1. Are you surprised to see that making an extra payment every month of *just* $10 can cut almost 10 years off of the time it takes to pay off a credit card bill depending upon the balance and interest rate?

2. If the power of *just* $10 excites, motivates, or inspires you, then go back to your spending journal and spending plan and see if there are any additional adjustments you can make to increase the amount of cash you create to go toward your debt elimination plan!

11.

Automatic Savings Accounts

It is not premature to talk about increasing the amount of savings that you have on hand before you write your debt elimination plan. Having at least $2,000 in a non-retirement savings account (i.e. short-term) will help you to not add to your debt while you are working hard to get rid of it. Having $2,000 will keep you from increasing your debt if you need emergency car repairs, such as tires or brakes, or if someone gets sick and there is a doctor visit copay and another copay for the prescription.

As you continue to review your daily spending in your journal, and you are adjusting your spending plan either monthly or each payday, you should already be seeing where you can make adjustments and redirect some of your current spendings into savings. Until you have $2,000 in savings, you should split the cash you create between your savings account and your debt elimination plan. You can start with half and a half, but getting $2,000 in savings is more important because "life" will happen at some point during your debt elimination marathon.

It is critically important to always be building your savings! Automatically saving money has been a sanity saver for me! I opened several savings accounts with an online financial institution and then scheduled automatic transfers from my primary (local) checking account every payday into my multiple savings accounts. The transfers happen with no further effort on my part, and the money in the accounts grow automatically and out of my sight. Remember the old saying – out of sight, out of mind!

As part of your plan to get out of debt, you may want to consider setting up at least one automatic savings account, especially if you do not already have $2,000 in an accessible savings account. Yes, most online financial institutions will let you have more than one savings account (find institutions without fees!). A big key to making these accounts work for you is *not* to have debit cards for your online accounts.

I have given each of my savings accounts a name and pre-scheduled the transfer amount. For example, I have accounts dedicated to my mortgage, vacation, my sorority, and more. When it is time to pay for something that I have an account for, I simply go to the account and withdraw the amount I need! I love it because these accounts go on my spending plan as money going into savings instead of as a line item for an expense.

Because your focus is getting out of debt, start with up to two savings accounts and schedule a small automatic transfer amount. You can manually transfer money into the accounts as you create it in your spending journal to get you to the $2,000 mark faster. Once you reach the $2,000 goal through the combination of automatic and manual transfers, the account will continue to grow from the automatic transfers while you are focusing all of your extra money on your debt elimination plan.

In the event of a critical need, there is also the flexibility of combining money in the different online accounts to cover unexpected, required expenses without using credit. For example, the first week after moving into my house I had to get an emergency cleaning of my home ventilation system, the refrigerator died and needed replacing (it was 20 years old), and my car needed brakes. This was all in the same week, and just after paying all of the moving expenses! Just because I wrote this book does not mean that I am excluded from life's "stuff". Stuff happens to me too – just like everyone one else! I encourage you to set up your automatic savings account now, and then add more accounts and more money later. Over time, your money will grow beyond the initial $2,000 and be there when you want it – and when you need it!

Most Americans do not save enough money each month. We all need accessible short-term accounts like the automatic savings accounts. However, we all also need long-term savings for retirement, college tuition, senior living care, etc. Long-term savings needs are best planned with the guidance of licensed, professional financial advisors. Not having enough savings can actually add to your debt if you do not have a financial safety net to draw from if and when an unexpected financial necessity arises. If you are scratching your head trying to figure out how you can save money at the same time that you have more bills than income, do not stress about it. Just like many other actions in this book, growing your savings is a process that you will work towards.

This book is about implementing several small actions at the same time and watching them come together over time to make a BIG difference in your life! Dr. Martin Luther King, Jr. said, *"faith is taking the first step even when you don't see the whole staircase"*. Have faith in yourself and keep moving through the processes in this book.

Find a reputable online financial institution that does not have savings account fees and open one or two savings accounts. Remember to use a secure internet connection, even if you have to use the connection at a friend or family member's house. I strongly suggest using an online financial institution, and not your current financial institution or a local financial institution. The best way to save money is to transfer it automatically to an inconvenient, not-easy-to-get-to location that also does not have debit card access! If you cannot walk into a branch and you do not have a debit card, you cannot easily access your money. This is how it grows instead of being spent at the mall, at your favorite eatery, or just disappearing.

Open the online savings account *without* a debit card and follow their instructions for linking your new account to your current primary account that you pay your bills from. Once the online account is open and linked to your primary account, you should be able to instantly open additional savings accounts within the initial online account. There should not be an issue linking an online account with your current primary bank or credit union. If you have trouble opening the online account or linking it to your primary account, call both the online bank and your current bank or credit union for help.

When the online savings account is open and linked to your primary account, set up an automatic transfer to happen every pay day. I suggest starting with two online savings accounts. One account will grow to the $2,000 you are setting aside to help keep you from adding to your debt if a true emergency arises. The second account will be used for end of year gift giving (if applicable). Schedule a transfer of at least $10 to each account each pay day for a starting minimum savings of $20 per paycheck. Give your accounts names that make you smile and reflect the purpose of the account – perhaps "not gonna use credit", "holiday shopping fun", "incredibly fabulous vacation", or "kids' field trips/college applications", etc.

If you have been faithfully updating your spending plan and using your spending journal, and you find that your money is still really tight, then schedule the $10 transfer into one account one pay day, and then $10 into the other account on the next payday for a total of $20 per month instead of $20 per payday. To do that, use the calendar feature in your online savings account and schedule $10 for one account every four weeks matching up with your next scheduled paycheck. Next, schedule $10 to the second account every four weeks starting with the following paycheck. However, if you know that you either waste or leak money every pay period and do not have at least $2,000 in short-term savings, then automatically transfer $25 - $50 every payday to get to the $2,000 goal faster.

As part of your debt elimination process, it is important that you build your short-term, on hand savings at the same time so that you have options other than taking on additional debt if or when unexpected major expenses happen. When you set up your online savings accounts, celebrate your victory! It is one of many small victories during your marathon to becoming debt free!

Money Savings Tip:

There is a huge opportunity for some readers to breathe easier financially each month. If your rent or mortgage payment is more than half of one paycheck and you pay the full amount out of that one check, that big expense does not leave much money until the next paycheck, especially if you have another expense that needs to be paid from the same check. For example, if your paycheck is $1,500 and your rent or mortgage is $1,000, then you only have $500 to stretch for two weeks until your next paycheck. That only leaves $500 for groceries, transportation, caring for your children, and other necessities.

If that is your situation, consider opening another online savings account just for your rent or mortgage, *and nothing else*. The goal is to automatically transfer half of your rent or mortgage into that account every pay day. That will allow you to have your full rent or mortgage payment in the bank every month while having more money available to live on throughout the month!

In the example above, if your rent or mortgage is $1,000, you would automatically transfer $500 from every paycheck into your online account that is only dedicated to your rent/mortgage. That would leave you with $1,000 from every paycheck to live on instead of only $500 when the rent or mortgage is due! You would pay your rent or mortgage directly from your online account, or transfer the payment amount back to your primary account and pay it from there. Here is a visual of the example:

You Now Every Month	
Pay 1	**Pay 2**
$1,500	$1,500
− $1,000 rent/mort	− (all bills)
$ 500 living	??? living

Your Possibility Every Month	
Pay 1	**Pay 2**
$1,500	$1,500
− $ 500 rent/mort	− $ 500 rent/mort
$1,000 bills and living	$1,000 bills and living

If this is appealing to you, it will take some work to get started but it will be well worth it! To make your possibility into *your reality*, you have to start by saving half of your rent or mortgage amount in your online rent/mortgage account while still paying all of your bills at the same time including your rent/ mortgage. I know it sounds a little far-fetched and it really is a stretch, but you can do it!

Here's how to *turn your possibility into your reality.* Use your spending plan and your spending journal to find money to add to your rent/mortgage account. Build that account balance to half of your rent/mortgage amount ($500 in my example), plus $5 to keep from having a zero balance after each monthly rent or mortgage payment is made (total of $505 in my example). Once you have half of a payment plus $5, schedule the automatic transfers every pay day in the amount that is half of your rent or mortgage amount. Since you already have saved half the amount, as soon as you start the transfers you will have the full amount in the bank when the next rent or mortgage payment is due!

Congratulations! Now you have more money to live on every pay day! If you choose to start using the rent/mortgage account, make sure you go back and adjust your monthly spending plan so that you reflect the extra money going into the rent/mortgage savings account every pay day.

If you find this *Money Savings Tip* a little confusing, understand that it is not part of your debt elimination plan. However, since it is a tip that could help you to breathe easier, please read it again. If you still do not understand it, ask a friend or simply keep paying your rent or mortgage the way you currently are.

A.S.A.P.
Action Steps toward your Action Plan

1. Open an online savings account with a financial institution that does not charge fees, and allows multiple accounts within the primary savings account. Do not request a debit card for the account!

2. Link the online savings account to your primary local bank or credit union account.

3. Within your online savings account, open an additional savings account. Give each account a name so you can tell them apart and know the purpose for each. It is your option whether you want to open a third savings account dedicated to your rent/mortgage as described in this chapter.

4. Schedule automatic transfers every pay day from your local account to your online accounts.

NOTE: If you need to access the money in your online savings account, simply follow the instructions to transfer the money back to your primary account. Know that it may take 2 – 3 business days for the transfer back to your primary account to take place.

12.

Writing Your Personalized

Debt Elimination Plan

Now that you have put your preliminary action steps for success into motion, it is time for you to start writing your personal debt elimination plan. I hope you are excited! This is where everything you have done so far in this book comes together to focus you on an accelerated, systematic plan to get out of debt. The systematic process for getting out of debt has been around for decades. However, it was made popular by Dave Ramsey[3] in the early 1990's when he coined the term *debt snowball*.

All of the pages and exercises in this book have been preparing you for this moment, which is to write your personalized debt elimination plan. Your debt elimination plan will be your blueprint for getting out of debt as quickly as possible. At this point, the four (4) steps to a debt free life that you should have completed are:

1. A written list of your debts from reviewing the last six months of your checkbook register and from your credit report. The list includes who you owe and your total outstanding balance

---

[3] Name is registered with the US Patent and Trademark Office

2. A written spending plan that you are using to track your income and expenses either every pay day or every month
3. Your spending journal that you are using to track your daily spending, and are using to create extra cash that you can apply to your debt elimination plan
4. Savings account with automatic transfers to start building your short-term savings to the minimum goal of $2,000

Once your personal debt elimination plan is created, you will systematically pay off your bills one at a time. There are only five (5) easy steps for creating your personal debt elimination plan – it is that simple! You will follow the steps outlined in the next few pages to identify which bill you will pay off first, and then determine the order you will follow to pay off your remaining bills.

Your plan is personalized by you, for you, and it is based solely upon your debts. If you are married, you and your spouse need to decide if you will have one joint debt elimination plan or two separate plans. If you choose two plans, be very clear about how any joint bills (i.e. shared credit cards, mortgage, etc.) will be listed in each plan, and how the money will be allocated to pay down and eliminate joint bills.

The only debts that go into your plan are debts that can be paid down to zero and not come back. Examples of debts include credit cards, loans, medical bills, car note (purchased, not leased), mortgage, etc. Examples of bills include utilities, cable, insurance, phone, etc. Bills get paid in full when they are due, and then recur on a regular basis.

Step 1:

To write your debt elimination plan, you can use paper and pencil or a spreadsheet software such as Microsoft® Excel®. For Step 1, write or type five columns with these labels at the top of each column (see Figure #1):

A) Creditor Name
B) Total Outstanding Balance
C) Minimum Payment (requested by your creditor)
D) Actual Payment (that you pay to your creditor)
E) Difference (your actual payment amount minus the minimum required payment)

Next, in the **Creditor Name** column, list the name of each creditor that you owe. These are the debts that you will be paying down to zero and eliminating. In the **Total Outstanding Balance** column, list the total outstanding amount of each debt as of your last payment, and write the minimum payment amount due that is listed on your statement in the **Minimum Payment Column**. If your minimum payment due varies, you will need to verify the amount each month. If you know that any of your minimum payments will be increasing soon, write in the higher amount.

The **Actual Payment** is the amount you actually paid on each bill. Often people round up a payment. For example, if the minimum payment is $148.96, many people will pay $150. Therefore, $150 is the actual payment and would be written in the column. If the amount you actually pay varies every month, then write in the average amount you paid in the past six months.

You may want to grab a calculator or your phone for the last column. Subtract the **Minimum Payment** (your 3rd column) from the **Actual Payment** (your 4th column) and write that amount in the **Difference** column. See Figure #1 for an idea of what your paper or spreadsheet should look like.

Figure #1

Step 1: List each debt including the Creditor Name, Total Balance, Minimum Payment, Actual Payment, and the Difference between the minimum and the actual payments				
A	**B**	**C**	**D**	**E**
Creditor Name	Total Balance	Minimum Payment	Actual Payment	Difference
				D – C = E

Step 2:

For Step 2, sort your table based upon the **Total Balance** (your 2nd column). You want your debt with the smallest outstanding **Total Balance** to be on the top line and your debt with the largest outstanding balance on the last line. The largest outstanding balance is usually your mortgage but maybe a car loan, student loan, or medical bill. If you are using paper, you will have to rewrite your columns with the debts in the correct order. On your new sheet of paper, make sure you fill in all five columns for each debt. See Figure #2.

Figure #2

A	B	C	D	E
	Step 2: Sort your list and put the debt with the smallest balance at the top of your list			
A	**B**	**C**	**D**	**E**
Creditor Name	Total Balance	Minimum Payment	Actual Payment	Difference
	Smallest			D – C = E
	to			
	Largest			

Step 3:

For Step 3, add the amounts in your *Difference* column (your 5ᵗʰ column) and write the total at the bottom of the column. This is the amount you currently are actually overpaying on your debts every month. For the purposes of your debt elimination plan, this extra amount is your monthly overpayment that you will start putting toward systematically getting out of debt. See Figure #3. If you pay every bill to the penny every month and the *Column Total* for *Difference* is zero, do not be discouraged because your personal debt elimination plan will still work!

Figure #3

Step 3: Add the amounts in the Difference column				
A	**B**	**C**	**D**	**E**
Creditor Name	Total Balance	Minimum Payment	Actual Payment	Difference
	Smallest			+
				+
	to			+
				+
	Largest			+
				= Column Total (CT)

Step 4:

Step 4 is where the action toward *you getting out of debt starts!* I hope you are excited! Take the **Column Total** for the **Difference** column (your 5th column) and add it to the first debt listed under **Minimum Payment** (your 3rd column), which is your debt with the smallest outstanding balance. This is the amount you will pay each month on your debt with the lowest balance until it is eliminated. Additionally, you will pay the **Minimum Payment** amount due on each of your other debts, and also pay your bills that are not in your debt elimination plan. See Figure #4.

Make sure you check the **Minimum Payment** amount due each month on each of your debts in case the amount changes. If the amount changes, make sure you pay the correct minimum amount and adjust both your debt elimination plan and your spending plan accordingly. Also remember to pay your bills on time because, as stated in chapter 5, consistent on-time payments will increase your credit scores, especially as your debt balances start decreasing.

Figure #4

Step 4: Add the Column Total (CT) to the minimum payment for your smallest bill and pay that amount. Pay the minimum amount due on all other bills on your list.

A	B	C	D	E
Creditor Name	Total Balance	Minimum Payment	Actual Payment	Difference
	Smallest	Amt + **CT**		D – C = E
		Pay minimum		
	to	Pay minimum		
		Pay minimum		
	Largest	Pay minimum		
				Column Total (CT)

Your debt with the smallest balance is what I call your **Bullseye Debt**. Your personal debt elimination plan will focus all of your attention on your **Bullseye Debt**. Figure 5 is an example of what your debt elimination plan should look like, except that you will write in the actual names of your creditors. Column F identifies the amount you will pay each month on each of your debts.

Figure #5

A	B	C	F	D	E
Creditor Name	Total Balance	Minimum Payment	What to Pay on Each Debt	Actual Payment	Difference
Credit Card #2	$321	$15.00	$15 + **$46.16**	$25	$10
Hospital Bill	$768	$15.00	$15.00	$15	$0
Credit Card #3	$1,229	$49.16	$49.16	$50	$0.84
Car Loan	$6,086	$343.00	$343.00	$350	$7
Credit Card #1	$7,124	$82.21	$82.21	$100	$17.79
Student Loan	$30,923	$284.96	$284.96	$284.96	$0
Mortgage	$167,208	$1,314.47	$1,314.47	$1,325	$10.53
					$46.16

In Figure 5, $46.16 is the Column Total for the Difference column, and it is added to the Minimum Payment for the ***Bullseye Debt*** on the first line which is Credit Card #2. Therefore, instead of paying $15 on Credit Card #2, the payment is $61.15 ($15 + $46.16).

Let's look at what the debt elimination plan does for paying off the debt in this example (assuming no interest or additional charges for the purpose of the illustration). If continuing to pay the Actual Payment of $25 per month, this $321 debt is paid off in just over one year at 12.84 months. If only paying the Minimum Payment of $15 per month, this $321 debt is paid off in almost two years at 21.4 months. However, by using the debt elimination plan and paying

$61.15 per month, this $321 debt is eliminated in just 5.25 months. This debt is eliminated 7 to 16 months early!

Wow! I hope this gets you excited about what the debt elimination plan can do for you! Did you notice in Figure #5 that some of the amounts in the Difference column are very small – less than $1? This is important because even with those low amounts, when everything is added together and then focused all onto one bill, the debt elimination plan cuts the time in debt on Credit Card #2 by more than 7 months! Know that no amount is too small to help you get out of debt faster! [Note: If you want to know how long it will take you to pay off your first bill, divide the Total Balance of your **Bullseye Debt** by the amount you are about to start paying.]

I hope the Figures and examples help you to understand the basics that you need to write your personal debt elimination plan. If you are not clear on something, I encourage you to read this chapter again because it is very important to me that you understand your debt elimination plan. However, if you do not fully understand it, do the work anyway and trust the process because the plan will still work!

Step 4 1/2:

What you have written so far is only the *start* of your debt elimination plan. You are not finished! I am calling this step 4 1/2. Here is where you will pour gasoline on the fire and *get out of debt even faster* by adding, even more, money to your monthly **Bullseye Debt** payment! The extra money you are about to add to your **Bullseye Debt** payment is coming from your spending journal, your spending plan, and any other extra income sources you have identified. This is why doing the early exercises in this book are so important for you!

The more money you created in the earlier chapters from within your current income sources, the faster you will get out of debt, especially if you stay focused! You can set the money you created aside (i.e. move it into a savings account) and then add it to your monthly *Bullseye Debt* payment when you pay your bills. Or, you can make additional payments on your *Bullseye Debt* throughout the month, each time you identify available money. Remember to check to make sure there are no extra fees for making multiple payments on the same bill in the same month. Also, make sure that all of your payments made during the billing cycle are equal to or more than the required minimum payment amount.

As you are implementing your debt elimination plan, if you find yourself making more than the Minimum Payment on any debts other than your *Bullseye Debt*, then you still have extra money that you should be adding to your *Bullseye Debt* payment. Literally, every penny counts when getting out of debt! Therefore, redirect every extra cent to your *Bullseye Debt* because consistently doing this will get you out of debt even faster!

Step 5:

Step 5 is where you really start to see your debts disappear! Figure 6 shows how the extra $61.16 eliminates your *Bullseye Debt*. You will eliminate your *Bullseye Debt* even faster because you will be adding extra money to each payment because you have been consistently using your spending journal (shown as "+ SJ") and updating your spending plan.

Figure #6

A	B	C	F	D	E
Creditor Name	Total Balance	Minimum Payment	What to Pay on Each Debt	Actual Payment	Difference
Credit Card #2	$321	$15.00	$15 + $46.16 + SJ*	$25	$10
Hospital Bill	$768	$15.00	$15.00	$15	$0
Credit Card #3	$1,229	$49.16	$49.16	$50	$0.84
Car Loan	$6,086	$343.00	$343.00	$350	$7
Credit Card #1	$7,124	$82.21	$82.21	$100	$17.79
Student Loan	$30,923	$284.96	$284.96	$284.96	$0
Mortgage	$167,208	$1,314.47	$1,314.47	$1,325	$10.53
					$46.16

*SJ is the extra cash created using your spending journal

Once your first debt is eliminated, cross it off and celebrate your success! *You did it! You paid off your first debt in record time!* Are you as excited as I am? I encourage you to celebrate this major milestone with your marathon to living a debt free life! For your celebration, you may choose to treat yourself to something special. If you decide to do something like eat out or have an extra movie night, plan a spending limit of about $25 so that you have fun celebrating while staying on track financially. Also, make sure you post your success on all of your favorite social media pages using the hashtag **#bullseyedebtbook**. This will allow the community of people reading this book to celebrate with you!

Here are more things for you to celebrate...not only will you have eliminated your first debt, but you will also have eliminated any doubts or negative self-talk in your mind about whether or not the debt elimination plan will work for you! Another huge benefit for you to celebrate and take advantage of is that you now have momentum and excitement to keep you charging forward to eliminate your remaining debts!

Since you have eliminated your first debt, there is a new debt on your top line in the *Bullseye Debt* elimination position. In our example in Figure #6, credit card #2 would now have a zero balance and be eliminated. That means the hospital bill is now on the top line in the *Bullseye Debt* position. This is where you have the opportunity to further customize your personal debt elimination plan.

It was very intentional to have you eliminate your debt with the smallest balance first. It was important to give you a sense of accomplishment and, for any naysayers, to prove that the debt elimination plan will work for you. Now that all of these things have been accomplished, you have a choice to make. It is your choice to continue with your personal debt elimination plan as is and eliminate your debts by always having your debt with the smallest outstanding balance in the *Bullseye Debt* elimination position. Or, you can choose to move a different bill into the *Bullseye Debt* elimination position.

Figure #7 shows you what you need to do next after you have eliminated your first debt and have chosen your next *Bullseye Debt.*

Figure #7

A	B	C	F	D	E
Creditor Name	Total Balance	Minimum Payment	What to Pay on Each Debt	Actual Payment	Difference
Credit Card #2			~ ELIMINATED ~		$10
Hospital Bill	$768	$15.00	$15.00 + **61.16** + **SJ**	$15	$0
Credit Card #3	$1,229	$49.16	$49.16	$50	$0.84
Car Loan	$6,086	$343.00	$343.00	$350	$7
Credit Card #1	$7,124	$82.21	$82.21	$100	$17.79
Student Loan	$30,923	$284.96	$284.96	$284.96	$0
Mortgage	$167,208	$1,314.47	$1,314.47	$1,325	$10.53
					$46.16

*SJ is savings journal

Remember that in Figure #6, $61.16 ($15 + $46.16) + SJ was the amount being paid on the first ***Bullseye Debt***, plus the extra money from your spending journal. Now that the first bullseye debt has been eliminated, the full $61.16 that was being applied to the first debt is now available to pay on your new ***Bullseye Debt*** (figure #7). This extra money is now added to the Minimum Payment and will eliminate the new ***Bullseye Debt*** much faster!

Some people believe all debts should be eliminated in order based upon the smallest outstanding balance. Others believe that the debt with the highest interest rate; or the most costly penalties; or the highest fees should be eliminated first. Then, there are those who believe that the debt that stresses you out the most should be your next choice as your **Bullseye Debt**. The "stress bill" is the bill that just the sight of the envelope in the mailbox or the thought of the bill raises your blood pressure and/or creates negative emotions.

There is no right or wrong answer regarding what bill you choose to move into the **Bullseye Debt** elimination position after you have eliminated your first debt because you are certain that the debt elimination system works. There is no right or wrong answer because the debt elimination system works regardless of what debt is in the **Bullseye Debt** position. It is time for you to choose your next **Bullseye Debt!**

If the thought of getting rid of your most stressful debt excites you, then you may choose to move it into the **Bullseye Debt** elimination position ahead of debts with smaller balances and/or higher interest rates. However, the debt elimination system only works when you focus all of your money and energy on one debt at a time while making the minimum payments on all of your other debts. If you focus on more than one debt at a time by paying more than the minimum amount due on more than one bill, then you will slow down your debt elimination process.

Now it is your turn to decide which way you will go with your next **Bullseye Debt**: smallest balance, highest interest rate, or your emotional stress bill. This is where your personal debt elimination plan becomes the most personal! You may choose to pay off the second debt based upon the smallest balance and then move to the highest interest rate or the emotional debt into the **Bullseye Debt** elimination position for your next bill. The important thing to remember is that the debt elimination system works. You have to create your debt elimination plan, stick with it, and use your spending journal and spending plan to create extra cash so you can get out of debt faster!

When your second **Bullseye Debt** is paid off, add the full amount of that payment to the Minimum Payment of your next **Bullseye Debt**. As you eliminate your debts, the money available to add to the minimum payment on the next **Bullseye Debt** will keep increasing, and it will keep accelerating your goal of getting out of debt! Remember to share your success after you eliminate each debt on social media using the hashtag **#bullseyedebtbook** so that our community can continue celebrating with you!

A.S.A.P.
*Action **S**teps toward your **A**ction **P**lan*

Chapter 13 is the meat of this book, with the chapters on spending plans and spending journals being your "secret sauce" for getting out of debt faster. Since this chapter is the meat of the book, for this A.S.A.P., please reread this chapter as many times as you need to write your personal debt elimination plan!

There are apps and websites available that will create your debt elimination plan for you. However, first, I always believe that it is best for you to do your own work so that you fully understand the process. Second, I do not know if the apps and websites allow you to customize your debt elimination plan and do things like move your "stress bill" into your *Bullseye Debt* elimination position. As I stated before, if you choose to use an app or website – do your research, including the amount of security/encryption provided.

Money Savings Tip:

After you have eliminated each credit card debt and have a zero balance, either close the credit card account or write the creditor and tell them to lower your credit limit. Since your balance is zero and your savings accounts are growing, you should not have to use your credit cards as often, if at all. Therefore, get rid of any possible temptation by closing the account or reducing your available credit limit. Debt free is going to be your new lifestyle!

13.

Handling Challenges During Your Debt Elimination Plan

I hope you are as excited as I am about the progress you have made so far and at all of the great options and opportunities that will be on your financial horizon as your debt decreases and your savings increases! As I have mentioned throughout this book, getting out of debt is a marathon, not a sprint. Therefore, since a marathon is 26.2 miles, I would like you to fully commit 26 months to doing (taking action!) everything you have read in this book so far.

Who knows, you may be debt free in less than 26 months using your personalized debt elimination plan. However, depending on how much debt you have it is possible for you to need 3 – 5 years or more to eliminate all of your debt. That is still exciting because you now have the confidence that getting out of debt is a realistic, attainable goal that you *will achieve* because you have a systematic, written plan in place as your guide.

It is also very realistic that you may face financial challenges while following your debt elimination plan. Your car may completely die, you may have a major expense, or your income may change. If you face a challenge that exceeds the amount you have in your online savings accounts, then you may be forced to take on new debt. However, if that happens you should be confident that you have the tools you need to adjust and get right back on track!

If you have to take on new debt (or add to your current debt), be conscious about how much debt you take on and if you need to adjust the order of your **Bullseye Debts.** If you need to quickly increase your savings, you can make adjustments for that as well by making the minimum payments on all of your bills for a few months and putting the Column Total for your Difference column and the money created from your spending journal into your savings until your savings reaches your target amount.

What I am about to mention is not a true financial challenge, but it can create one. You have firmly committed to getting out of debt. Therefore, you absolutely must be mindful of impulsive spending and spending that you did not plan for. Do not let *SALE* become a 4-letter word that knocks you off of your plan and keeps you in debt longer! You need to weigh the impact of any impulsive, unplanned purchases against your overall goal. You may want to wait at least 3 days before making impulsive purchases to really decide if you *need* the item, especially if you are going to add to your debt to make the purchase. Remember the power of *just* $10 on accelerating you getting out of debt. You do not want a series of $10 purchases (that $175 jacket you have been watching is now *on sale* for $100!) adding to your debt and thereby keeping you in debt months and even years longer!

The key to handling financial challenges is to strategically use your spending plan and your spending journal in ways to create the cash you need to most effectively address any challenge you may face. As you get more and more comfortable with using the tools and resources in this book, you will become more and more comfortable with handling your money and making sound day-to-day financial decisions. There may come a day when you find yourself laughing because you are excited about using your spending plan and spending journal to create extra cash to pay for something without going into debt. Or, you may use those tools to make an informed decision to go into debt because you calculated exactly how fast you will pay it off. Yes, the same two tools that may have stressed you out a few chapters ago will become your "go to" resources for staying out of debt!

14.

Yes, You Can!

You made it to the end of the book! I hope you are excited about the steps you have already taken toward getting out of debt, and your next steps! I know that it is a lot of work – I am not trying to sugar coat it. However, the work-to-reward ratio is extremely high! Now that you have read the book and started doing the work, go back and revisit the answers you wrote down in chapter 3 as the answers to these questions:

1. Why do you want to get out debt? To get to the real root reason, ask yourself "why" to whatever you first write down, and then write your second answer. Ask yourself "why" to your second and subsequent answers and you may be surprised by the reason that hiding deep down inside of you!

2. How will you feel when you pay off your last targeted bill and all of your unwanted debt is gone?

I pray that when you read your answers now, you are filled with optimism, excitement, and happiness as you dream toward your debt free date and your debt free lifestyle! Why? Because you have a personal debt elimination plan in writing, and the knowledge and information needed to see it through to completion!

This book is jam packed with information and I hope you choose to follow each and every step and choose to complete each and every action item. Due to the amount of information in the book, let me quickly summarize your *5 SIMPLE Steps to a Debt Free Life* you now have to create your personalized debt elimination plan, although there are several supporting action items:

- ✓ *List your creditors:* Step 1 – Know who you owe and how much you to each creditor (include money owed that may not be on your credit report)

- ✓ *Write (and use) a spending plan:* Step 2 – Create a spending plan (budget) so that you can track your income and expenses

- ✓ *Write (and use) a spending journal:* Step 3 – Use a spending journal daily for at least 60 days, but preferably until you are debt free. Write every purchase you make every day in your spending journal and look for opportunities to make adjustments and redirect the money to your *Bullseye Debt*

- ✓ *Set up an automatic savings account:* Step 4 – Open a separate savings account (online is usually easiest), schedule automatic transfers on your paydays, and save at least $2,000 for unexpected expenses so that you do not add to your debt while you are working to eliminate your current debt. Open a second account with automatic transfers if you purchase end of year gifts so that you do not add to your debt each year. Get a copy of my first book, *12 Ways to Put Money in Your*

Pocket Every Month Without A Part-Time Job for great tips on gift buying and much more

✓ ***Write your debt elimination plan:*** Step 5 – Read, reread, and follow the 5 steps detailed in chapter 12 to write your debt elimination plan. Identify your debt with the smallest balance and focus any and all extra money on this debt, your ***Bullseye Debt.*** When your first debt is paid off, add that money to the minimum payment of your next ***Bullseye Debt***

✓ Personalize your debt elimination plan: After you pay off your debt with the smallest balance, identify which debt you will pay off second and the order for paying off your remaining debts. Revisit your spending journal regularly to see if you can identify extra cash to redirect to your ***Bullseye Debt***

✓ Join my mailing list at www.BullseyeDebtBook.com. Periodically I send a newsletter with financial tips and other valuable information. Plus, I give away some really good financial information to everyone who signs up

You now have the basic tools and resources to successfully start, act upon, and then finish your marathon journey to living a debt free life! Just think of what your life will be like as your stress level decreases because your debt is decreasing…and then you make that final payment on your last debt! There you have it! And, you can still enjoy some of the life's pleasures along the way with limited, *planned* spending!

I look forward to hearing from you along your journey to becoming debt free! Please post your testimonies on my Facebook page, https://www.facebook.com/JennSMatthews/ or send them to me at Jennifer@JenniferSMatthews.com. Also, as you just read, sign up for my mailing list at www.BullseyeDebtBook.com so that you will get tips and motivation from me along your journey (marathon) to becoming debt free.

Bonus Point #1

How To Get Two Extra Paychecks Every Year!

If you get paid every other week, then two months out of each year you get three (3) paychecks. Since you are used to living on two paychecks per month for 10 months out of the year, these two months with an extra check present a great opportunity for extra cash to split between your debt elimination plan and your savings!

Grab a calendar and mark your pay days until you come to the months with three checks. Those months are about six (6) months apart. The key to finishing these months with an extra check is your spending plan! For each of these months, you literally need to plot out which bills you are paying from which paychecks. You want to spread your payments out across the three paychecks while being mindful of the due dates for each bill.

If your net paycheck is $1,500, you want to see how you can plan your bills and expenses so that you can have as close to $1,500 at the end of the month as you can. It is very unlikely that your planning will allow you to finish evenly at $500, $500, and $500 per paycheck. Your results may look like: $250, $600, and $650 remaining from each paycheck. Or, to maintain on time bill payment, you may end the month with $1,000 and be a little short of the full paycheck goal. However, being able to finish with an extra $1,000 would be more than you have had left over in your previous months with three paychecks!

Saving one paycheck during each of those two months of the year only works if you carefully plan your spending in the months that have a third paycheck. Once you have the extra money, regardless of the amount, you can decide how you want to divide it between your **Bullseye Debt** and your savings.

Bonus Point #2

To Pay Off My Mortgage or Not Pay Off My Mortgage – That is the Question!

There are several schools of thought as to whether or not people should pay off their mortgages. Since I do not give tax, financial, or real estate advice, I will give you my opinion and then refer you to your tax and financial professionals for advice. When you speak with them, you should have a few questions for the conversations based on this Bonus Point.

Here is my opinion about paying off mortgages...most people should not keep a mortgage just for the tax write-off, even pre-retirement. Everyone will hit a point during the life of their mortgage when the amount of interest paid that can be written off on your taxes is probably not worth keeping the mortgage just for the tax write-off. What do I mean? Look at the amortization table you received as part of your settlement papers.

The first several years of your mortgage payments consist of more of your money going to interest than to principal, and the interest may be deductible if you file the IRS Schedule A or other tax forms. Then, you will reach a point when the percentage of interest to principal paid is about 50/50. After that, your tax deductions decrease because you have reached the point where you are paying more toward your principal than to your interest.

As an example, let's say you have been in your house for a while. Your mortgage payment is $1,000 per month, with $900 going to principal and $100 per month going to interest that may be tax deductible. In this example, you would be paying $12,000 (12 monthly payments of $1,000) to potentially write off $1,200 ($100 in interest for 12 months). If you did not have a mortgage, in this example you would have an extra $12,000 in your pocket with no mortgage payment. You would still have to pay real estate taxes out of the $12,000, and then you would have money left over to potentially offset any increase in tax liability, add to your retirement, use for vacation, and much more.

I do not give tax, investment, and/or legal advice. Therefore, I recommend that if you have a mortgage that you speak with a Certified Public Accountant (CPA) regarding minimizing your tax liability, especially if you have reached the point in your mortgage payments that you are paying more toward your principal than toward interest. Ask your CPA if paying off your mortgage is the right option for you, what your tax liability will be, and alternatives to Schedule A such as a qualifying business on Schedule C.

In addition to speaking with a CPA, I also suggest speaking with a licensed financial advisor to see if it is beneficial for you to pay off your mortgage. A financial advisor can speak to you about your options for investing the amount of your monthly mortgage payment, and then either setting aside the potential tax liability or paying the tax liability from the anticipated return on your investment.

Again, I am not giving advice. Professionals in each of these areas will give you advice from their perspective (i.e. tax advantages and long-term investment goals). If you are not sure if paying off your mortgage is beneficial for you, then you should seek advice from the appropriate professionals. If you choose to pay off your mortgage, simply plug it into your debt elimination plan and then knock it out when it moves into the *Bullseye Debt* position!

About the Author

Jennifer S. Matthews is a sought after motivational and informational speaker who is known for her practical approaches for helping people "get it" when it comes to understanding and managing money. She is trained as a financial coach and speaks to a wide array of audiences, including corporations and community organizations. Visit her website, *www.PositiveFinancialImpactNOW.com* for resources and information that can help you have an immediate positive impact on your finances.

Jennifer is the best-selling, awarding-winning author of *12 Ways to Put Money in Your Pocket Every Month Without A Part-Time Job; The Skinny Book That Makes Your Wallet Fat.* The book was selected by the Institute for Financial Literacy as their 2012 Adult's Book of the Year, General and received their Excellence in Financial Literacy Education (EIFLE™) award. Jennifer earned a master's degree from LaSalle University and an MBA from Johns Hopkins University. She was a Delegate at the Global Summit on Financial Literacy and participated in the White House Office of Faith-Based and Community Initiatives Compass in Action Roundtable on Financial Literacy.

Jennifer has made numerous television and radio appearances, including being a regular guest financial expert on a consumer television show in Washington, DC for several years, and was a featured expert in a mini-documentary that aired on public television. Visit Jennifer online at *www.PositiveFinancialImpactNOW.com* where you can subscribe to her mailing list.

Author's Note:

My first book, ***12 Ways to Put Money in Your Pocket Every Month Without A Part Time Job; The Skinny Book That Makes Your Wallet Fat***, show readers how to create an average of $300 per month, every month. If you have not read that book (it has even fewer pages than this one!) you probably want to read it because it will help you create even more cash for you to use to accelerate the debt elimination plan you created using this book. The book is available online at *www.PositiveFinancialImpactNOW.com*, Amazon, Barnes and Noble, and other outlets.

Please remember to post your testimonies on my Facebook page. You are also invited to post a book review and/or testimony on Amazon.com.

MY DEBT FREE LIFE NOTES:

_____

_____

_____

_____

_____

_____

_____

_____

_____

_____

_____

_____

_____

MY DEBT FREE LIFE NOTES:

MY DEBT FREE LIFE NOTES:

MY DEBT FREE LIFE NOTES:

_____

_____

_____

_____

_____

_____

_____

_____

_____

_____

_____

_____

_____

MY DEBT FREE LIFE NOTES:

_____

_____

_____

_____

_____

_____

_____

_____

_____

_____

_____

_____

_____

Made in the USA
Middletown, DE
06 February 2017